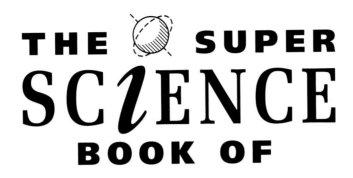

THE SUPER SCIENCE BOOK OF LIFE PROCESSES

David Glover

Eat, Sleep And Breathe It

Living is to breathe
Out and in
Never stopping
Never ceasing
Always drawing
Breath in,
Breathing life,
Out and in.

Living is to eat –
Bite and swallow.
Ever hunting
Ever feeding
Always needing
Food and water,
Gulping life down
With a bite and a swallow.

Living is to sleep
Dark and deep.
Half a life asleep,
Every muscle saving
And conserving
Energy to awake
Alive and living,
From the dark and deep.

by Lizzie Lewis

Illustrations by Frances Lloyd

Thomson Learning • New York

Books in the Super Science series

Energy
The Environment
Forces
Life Processes
Light
Materials

Our Bodies
Rocks and Soils
Sound
Space
Time
Weather

First published in the
United States in 1995 by
Thomson Learning
115 Fifth Avenue
New York, NY 10003

First published in Great Britain in 1994 by
Wayland (Publishers) Ltd.

Library of Congress Cataloging-in-Publication Data
Glover, David.
  The super science book of life processes / David Glover;
illustrations by Frances Lloyd.
      p.   cm. – (Super science)
  Includes bibliographic references (p. 47) and index.
  ISBN 1-56847-225-0
  1. Biology – Juvenile literature. 2. Life (Biology) – Juvenile
literature. [1. Life (Biology). 2. Biology] I. Lloyd, Frances, ill.
II. Title. III. Series.
QH309.2.G68   1994
574 – dc20   94-20898

Printed in Italy

Series editor: James Kerr
Designer: Loraine Hayes Design

Picture acknowledgments

Illustrations by Frances Lloyd
Cover illustration by Martin Gordon

Photographs by permission of: Bruce Coleman 11 (Dieter &
Mary Plage), 17 bottom (M P L Fogden), 25 (John Markham);
Mary Evans Picture Library 14; NHPA 5 bottom (Nigel
Dennis), 6 (M. I. Walker), 7, 9 top (A. P. Barnes), bottom
(Stephen Dalton), 10 top (Alain Compost), bottom (George
Bernard), 15 (Stephen Dalton), 18 (G. I. Bernard), 22
(Anthony Bannister), 23 (Stephen Dalton), 27 bottom (Roger
Tidman), 28 (Karl Switak); Oxford Scientific Films 5 top, 12
top (George I Bernard), 17 top (M Austerman), 21 (G A
Maclean); Tony Stone Worldwide 12 bottom (Geoff Dove),
20 (Fritz Prenzel); ZEFA 16, 26, 27.

CONTENTS

THE LIVING WORLD

The variety of life on earth is incredible. You are alive; a tree is alive; worms and maggots are alive; grass is alive; even the mold on a piece of stale bread is alive! From the simplest life form to the most complex, all living things are made up of cells, the basic unit of life. They also have other features in common: living things grow, feed, sense changes in their surroundings, reproduce young that grow to be like themselves, and, in time, grow old and die. These life processes make our world into a place of excitement and change.

To make sense of the huge variety of life on earth, scientists group all living things into five kingdoms – animals, plants, fungi, bacteria, and protists.

Bacteria and protists are the ▶ smallest life forms. Too small to be seen with the naked eye, they can be studied using a microscope. Bacteria and protists live everywhere: in soil, in the air, in water, even inside our bodies. Some bacteria cause disease, but others are useful, helping to digest food and keep our skin clean.

Some fungi are tiny, too. For example, the yeast that makes bread rise is a fungus. But a toadstool like the one below is just a small part of a much bigger fungus, most of which consists of long underground threads. In fact, a fungus discovered in California is thought to be the largest living thing on earth. It is more massive than a blue whale – the largest animal – or a giant redwood tree – the largest plant. ▼

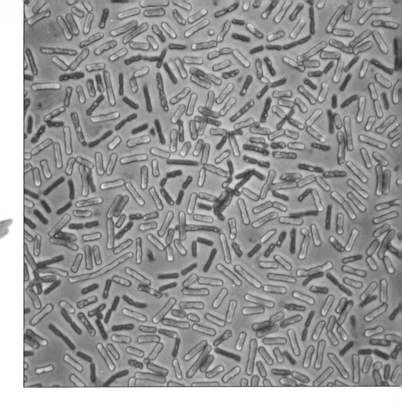

There are more than 350,000 plant species, but the animal kingdom is the largest and most varied kingdom of all. More than 1,500,000 animal species have been named, but there are up to 10,000,000 animal species that scientists have yet to discover and name. There are more than 2,000,000 species of insects alone!

BODIES

Building a body is a lot like building a house. There are countless ways to do it, but every house or body must have certain features. A house has to have a door; a body must have openings to take in food and air, and openings to pass out waste. A house must be strong enough to keep its shape in all kinds of weather and to protect its occupants; a body must keep its shape, too, and protect its delicate parts from bumps and infections.

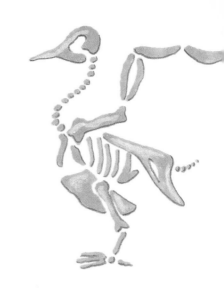

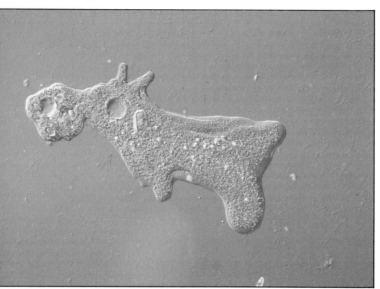

◀ Many small creatures have soft bodies held together inside a tough outer skin, or membrane, much like a balloon full of jelly. The soft body of an amoeba, a member of the protist kingdom, changes shape as it moves. The amoeba spreads part of its body, making a false foot to draw the rest of its body along.

Larger animals, and many small ones, have stiff skeletons to protect and support their bodies. Skeletons can be inside the body, like a tent frame, or on the outside, like the armor on a tank.

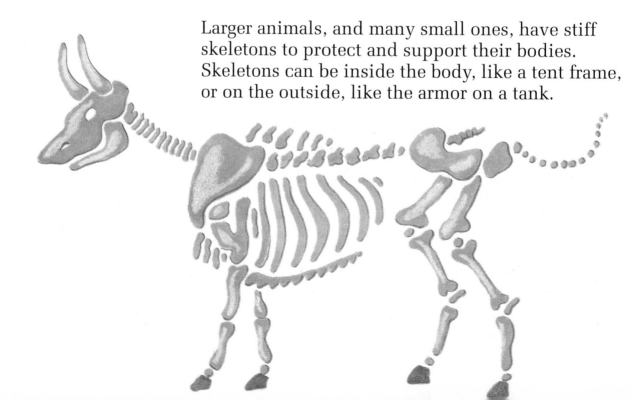

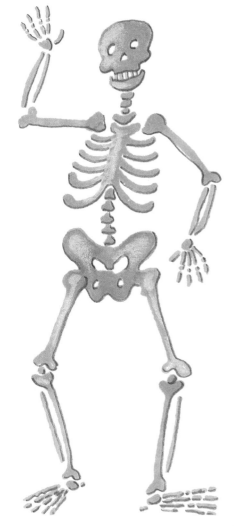

Some animals, such as insects and crabs, have a skeleton on the outside of their bodies. One problem with having a skeleton like a suit of armor is that it could prevent the animal from growing. This difficulty, however, is solved by molting. When a crab grows too big for its shell, the shell splits. For a few hours the crab's soft body is exposed to danger before its new, bigger shell hardens.

Fish, amphibians, reptiles, birds, and mammals have internal skeletons. The skeleton is a frame that supports the rest of the body. It is also a set of hinged levers operated by muscles to produce movement, and a cage that protects delicate organs.

◄ Stems of plants are stiffened with fibers of cellulose. They often take the form of hollow tubes, for lightness and strength. In bigger plants, more strength is needed. Trees produce a substance called lignin, which makes a tree trunk strong enough to withstand a gale.

WOW!
The human body contains 206 bones. The smallest is the stirrup bone in the ear, which is just one-tenth inch long in an adult. The largest is the thigh bone, or femur, which may be longer than 20 inches.

BREATHING

In the past it wasn't just polite to cover your mouth when you yawned – people believed that it also kept a devil from getting in with your breath! Now we know that yawning does us more good than harm. It empties stale air from our lungs and refills them with the fresh air we need to stay alert and active.

How long can humans live without air? If you are deprived of air for more than a few minutes, you will lose consciousness and soon die. But some mammals can go without breathing for long periods – a sperm whale can stay underwater for nearly two hours before surfacing for another breath of air. ▶

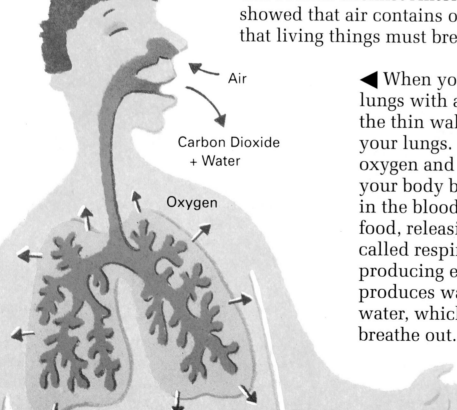

The French chemist Antoine-Laurent Lavoisier first showed that air contains oxygen. Oxygen is the gas that living things must breathe to survive.

Air

Carbon Dioxide + Water

Oxygen

◀ When you breathe in, filling your lungs with air, oxygen passes through the thin walls of tiny blood vessels in your lungs. Red blood cells collect the oxygen and are then pumped around your body by your heart. The oxygen in the blood combines with digested food, releasing energy. This process is called respiration. In addition to producing energy, respiration also produces waste carbon dioxide and water, which you get rid of when you breathe out.

Analyze your breath
You can detect the water in your breath by breathing onto a cold surface. The water condenses into a film of droplets. ▶

◀ All living things respire to produce energy. But they don't all take oxygen from the air in the same way. Mammals, birds, amphibians, and reptiles have lungs. But insects take in oxygen through holes, called spiracles, in their hard outer bodies. Plants have similar holes called stomata on the underside of their leaves.

How can plants and animals get oxygen under water? Oxygen dissolves in water in much the same way that sugar dissolves in tea. So oxygen is available underwater if your body is designed to extract it. Fish and most young amphibians do this with feathery gills. These tadpoles' gills are on either side of the head. ▶

◀ Why do we eat? Apart from giving us pleasure, food is fuel. It provides us with the energy our bodies need to work. But that's not the whole story; food is also building material. It contains the raw materials that are needed for bodies to grow and repair themselves, patching up and replacing parts that are old or damaged.

All the energy that is stored in ▶ food comes from the energy in sunlight. Plants are the only living things that can trap this energy directly. When sunlight falls on a plant's green leaves, a process called photosynthesis takes place. Inside the leaves, a green substance called chlorophyll traps light energy, causing carbon dioxide from the air and water taken up by the roots to combine to make sugars. These sugars are life's fuel both for the plants that produce them and for the animals that eat the plants.

Animals cannot trap light energy directly, so they must eat plants or other animals to build and fuel their bodies. Plant eaters such as the giraffe are called herbivores. Meat eaters such as the lion are called carnivores.

▲ Small, fast-moving creatures need a lot of energy; they spend nearly their whole time feeding. A hummingbird feeds on the energy-rich nectar provided by flowers. Larger, slower creatures need relatively less energy; they can be more lazy. A three-toed sloth spends sixteen hours a day asleep and another two hours dozing!

Plants get their energy from sunlight, but where do they obtain the materials to build their bodies? The answer is from the soil. They take up essential elements such as nitrogen and phosphorus through their roots. Animals need more than just energy, too. The correct balance of proteins, carbohydrates, minerals, and vitamins is essential to build up and maintain a healthy body.

WOW!
A pygmy shrew must eat more than its own weight of worms every day to supply its high-energy lifestyle.

SENSING

Some flowers open during the day, ▶ but close at night. Plants are sensitive to light, and respond by growing toward the sun. Plants can sense direction as well; their stems grow up while their roots grow down.

Animal senses are more developed than plant senses. Animals can detect many kinds of change in their environment. They respond to light, sound, gravity, heat, smells, vibrations, and, in some cases, electricity and magnetism.

All but the tiniest animals have a nervous system, which works like a telephone network, carrying signals from sense detectors such as the eyes and ears along nerves to the brain. The brain decodes the signals and sends messages back to the muscles to make the body respond.

▲ Eyes detect light. The primitive eyes of a clam are little more than pinholes, but they detect the shadows cast by potential predators. When this happens, the clam shuts its shell for safety.

◀ The compound eye of an insect has lenses facing in many directions so that the insect can spot danger approaching from all angles. You have to be sneaky and quick to swat a fly!

Experiment with your sense of touch

1 Shut your eyes and ask a friend to touch you with feathers. Can you tell whether it is one feather or two?
2 Try the experiment on the back of your hand, fingertips, forehead, and leg. You can feel the difference between one feather and two more easily with the sensitive body parts that have more nerve endings under the skin.

Many animals have better developed senses than humans. Dogs have a powerful sense of smell. Sniffer dogs can find explosives and drugs hidden in baggage.

A sense of balance keeps us standing ▶ up and enables some people to perform tricks such as riding a unicycle. Balance is sensed by the semicircular canals in our ears.

WOW!
Male moths use their feathery antennae to smell chemicals released by female moths up to 6 miles away!

13

MOVING

Most plants are rooted to one spot throughout their lives. They grow toward the light and may spread to find better soil, but they cannot get up and walk to a new home if the present one is unsuitable. Some small plants float freely at the surface of water, but they are swept wherever the currents or tide takes them.

One of the main differences between ▲ animals and plants is that animals can move in order to find food and shelter. On land, legs are a good way of getting around, though animals such as snakes and worms manage well by slithering and wriggling.

▲ A galloping horse can travel at 30 miles an hour. Before the invention of film, many people wondered about whether a horse ever has all four feet off the ground at the same time. Artists who painted galloping horses usually left one foot on the ground. The mystery was solved in 1877, when Eadweard Muybridge took the first photographs of moving horses. These showed that at some points all four feet are off the ground.

◀ Flying through the air must surely be the most wonderful way of getting around. Insects, birds, and bats fly by lifting themselves with wings that beat against the air. Throughout history, people have dreamed of flying like the birds. In a Greek legend, Daedalus and his son Icarus flew on wings made from feathers stuck together with wax. But Icarus flew too close to the sun, the wax melted, and he plummeted into the sea.

Good swimmers have streamlined bodies that travel through the water easily. The sailfish is probably the fastest swimmer of all. It can move at about 60 miles an hour in short bursts. ▶

WOW!
A species of millipede found in California has 750 legs.

STAYING ALIVE

Antarctica is one of the coldest places on earth. During the Antarctic winter, the sun never rises, the temperature falls to −60°F, and the wind blows at 100 miles an hour. Yet this is the time when emperor penguins lay their eggs and rear their young.

◄ How do they survive? Their bodies are adapted to cope with the conditions. A thick layer of blubber beneath their feathers insulates them from the cold. The penguins huddle together for extra warmth. Every few hours those on the outside of the huddle will squeeze to the middle. The penguins keep their eggs warm by balancing them on top of their feet and covering them with their feathered bellies.

Plants and animals can be found nearly everywhere on the earth, from the extreme cold of the Antarctic to the searing heat of the desert. Special adaptations like those of an emperor penguin allow one species of plant or animal to survive where another would soon die.

In the desert the keys to survival ► are conserving water and keeping cool. Desert cacti do not have leaves like other plants; their rounded shape reduces the surface area through which water is lost. Their thick, waxy skins also help to keep water in. Spines are an adaptation that help to protect the cactus from desert animals that chew it for the water it contains.

◀ Two animals that live in the hot climate of northern Africa share the same type of adaptation. The fennec fox has huge ears, not just to listen for prey, but also to keep it cool. As the fox's warm blood flows through its ears, heat escapes into the surrounding air. The elephant's ears do the same job – increasing the surface area through which the animal loses heat from its blood. When it is particularly hot, elephants flap their ears to cool their bodies.

▲ Many animals have adaptations that defend them from predators. Spines or a shell protect a soft body, while camouflage makes an animal difficult to spot. Bright warning colors tell a predator that the creature is bad to eat or poisonous. Sometimes warning colors are a fake. True coral snakes like the one in the photograph are very poisonous, but other species that mimic the coral snake's colors are not poisonous at all.

REPRODUCTION

When an organism matures, it reproduces, making new life from old and ensuring that the species is continued by the next generation. Your parents are the generation before you, your grandparents the generation before them. If you have children of your own, they will be the next generation.

Cells dividing

Some organisms reproduce by splitting themselves into parts. Bacteria divide in two; sea anemones can reproduce in this way, and so can many plants. A strawberry plant puts out runners that grow roots and develop into new plants. Because no mating is involved, this type of reproduction is called asexual. Asexual reproduction produces offspring that are exact copies, or clones, of the parent. ▼

DNA

◀ Sexual reproduction takes place when a male and a female of a species mate. The offspring have a mixture of both parents' features. A black cat that mates with a ginger male will have a litter of kittens, some of which are black, some ginger, and some tortoiseshell.

The features of one generation are carried into the ▶ next by a tiny thread of hereditary material called DNA. DNA is a code that, like a recipe, spells out exactly what the living thing is like. A piece of the DNA code that produces a particular result is called a gene. Human genes determine such things as the color of a person's hair, while plant genes decide whether a flower is pink or white, for example.

In sexual reproduction, the genes of the male and female are mixed together. Each baby takes half its genes from its mother and half from the father. But sometimes mistakes get made in the DNA, and the new generation may by chance have a feature that was not present in any previous generation.

If chance or random changes in a gene help the new generation to survive and reproduce, the changes are carried into future generations; eventually, a new species may appear. But changes that make it harder to survive soon vanish. This is called evolution. Billions of years of evolution have produced the fantastic variety of species that now inhabit the earth.

STARTING LIFE

A new life starts when a female egg cell is fertilized by a male sex cell. The genes in the two cells combine, and the fertilized egg develops into an embryo.

In mammals, fertilization takes place inside the mother's body. Male sperm cells enter the female's uterus during mating and fertilize one or more eggs. The embryos grow inside the uterus. They are supplied with oxygen and food through a cord connected to the mother's blood supply.

WOW!
The eggs of the sturgeon fish, called caviar, are a delicacy worth their weight in gold.

◀ When baby mammals are born they may be well developed, like a foal, or still quite helpless, like baby kangaroos. The mother feeds her babies on milk from her mammary glands. She continues to look after her young, for several years in the case of larger mammals, until they can fend for themselves.

Many plants can reproduce either by dividing asexually or by sexual reproduction. A flower such as a foxglove has both male and female parts. The anthers produce pollen grains, which contain male sex cells. The tiny pollen grains are carried from flower to flower by the wind, by insects, by birds, and in some cases ◄ by gardeners.

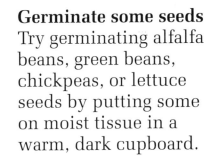

When a pollen grain from a plant lands on the female part of a flower of the same species, it fertilizes an egg cell, which develops into a seed. When the seeds are ready, they must be dispersed to a new patch of soil where they can grow. The seeds may just fall to the ground or they may have parts that act like wings or parachutes so that they travel on the wind. In some cases, seeds are eaten by an animal and then deposited in its droppings, or the seeds have hooks that catch in the fur of animals that pass by.

Germinate some seeds
Try germinating alfalfa beans, green beans, chickpeas, or lettuce seeds by putting some on moist tissue in a warm, dark cupboard.

When the temperature and moisture level are just right, a seed lying in the soil begins to grow and develop. This is called germination. The root appears first, followed shortly by the seed leaves. ▶

GROWING AND MATURING

Plants grow throughout their lives, but not at a steady rate. There is a definite growing season when the air is warm, there are many hours of sunlight, and the soil is moist. When winter comes, growth slows down. The pattern of growth is revealed by the growth rings in a tree trunk. Each ring records one year's growth, so we can tell the age of the tree by counting the number of rings it has. ▶

Like trees, reptiles never stop growing. Growth rings on a tortoise shell give its age in much the same way as growth rings in a tree.

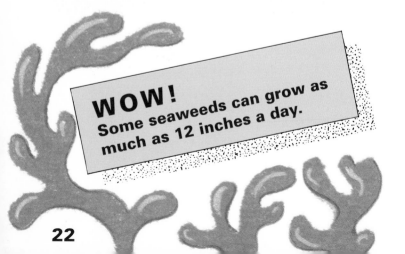

WOW!
Some seaweeds can grow as much as 12 inches a day.

Mammals, on the other hand, stop growing when they reach adulthood. A human infant grows most rapidly during the first six months of its life. From then on, growth gradually slows until the age of 12 to 14 when, for a short period during puberty, growth is more rapid again. Adult height is reached at 19 to 21 years.

A baby is not the same shape as an adult. Our body shape changes as we grow up, because our body parts grow at different rates. The head grows least, while the arms and legs grow most.

Over the centuries, the average height of adult humans has been increasing. If you look at furniture, clothing, and even suits of armor in museums, they all seem to have been made for small people. Modern people are taller because of improved diet and health.

▲ Insects such as butterflies, bees, and wasps do most of their growing as caterpillars or grubs. A butterfly egg is about the size of a pinhead. It hatches into a tiny caterpillar that feeds almost constantly, growing steadily until it is about 1 inch long and weighs 1,000 times more than when it hatched.

Then the caterpillar pupates, changing into a chrysalis. In the chrysalis the caterpillar's body changes completely. This process is called metamorphosis. In a few weeks the adult emerges. The adult butterfly does not grow any further.

LEARNING

Young animals have much to learn as they grow into adults. Many skills are learned by imitation. A young chimpanzee cannot crack a nut between two stones, but after watching an older chimp who has mastered the task, and with lots of practice, the baby will develop the knack. ▶

Think of all the things a child learns in the first few years of life before starting school: walking, talking, feeding, dressing, holding a pencil, throwing a ball. A two-year-old knows only a few words. By the time he or she is five, the child may know more than 3,000 words.

Konrad Lorenz was one of the first ▶ people to study animal learning and behavior scientifically. He found that when young geese (called goslings) hatch from their eggs, they think that the first creature they see is their mother. Lorenz called this behavior imprinting. The goslings follow their "mother" around even if it is really a human being.

Play is an important part of learning. Young cats develop their hunting skills in play fights with their brothers and sisters.

◀ This beautiful nest was built by wasps. How do small insects learn to make something so complicated? The answer is that wasps don't learn nest-building skills at all – they are born with them. Just as we don't learn to breathe, but do so instinctively as soon as we are born, nest building is instinctive to wasps. The wasps make the nests from paper, which they produce by mixing chewed wood with saliva to make a pulp.

Which animal is the most intelligent? It is difficult to judge the intelligence of other animals. One measure is the size of the brain compared to the size of the body; another is the difficulty of problems, such as finding hidden food, that the animal can solve. Reptiles are not very intelligent, but birds such as parrots and crows can learn quite complicated tasks. Of the mammals, the great apes – chimps, gorillas, and orangutans – are clearly very intelligent. Elephants are intelligent, too. But the sea mammals – dolphins and whales – have the biggest brains of all. Their brains are even bigger than human brains. ▼

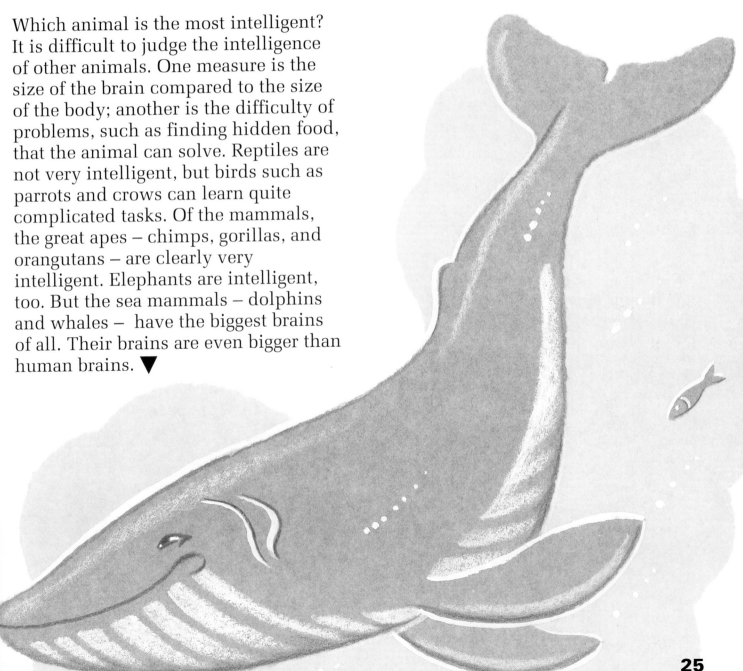

LIVING TOGETHER

▲ There's safety in numbers. Fish school, grazing mammals gather in huge herds, and birds flock in the thousands. Being a member of a large group provides protection from predators. By flocking together, animals can warn each other of approaching danger and perhaps confuse an attacker. It is usually a young or weak animal that cannot keep up with the others that falls prey to the hunter.

Up to 300 naked mole rats live together in an underground colony. In many ways, life in the colony is highly organized. Small worker mole rats dig tunnels and find food. Larger soldiers guard the colony from attack. The queen is the only female that reproduces. Every few hours she goes on patrol, sniffing the other rats to make sure they are not strangers. ▼

WOW!
Herds of more than 10,000,000 springbok gathered in southern Africa in the nineteenth century.

◀ A clown fish and a sea anemone work as partners. The clown fish is immune to the stinging cells in the anemone's tentacles, so it can live among anemones, protected from predators. In return for its safe home, the clown fish brings the anemone food and fights off other fish that might attack its partner. When two species live together in a way that benefits them both, it is called symbiosis.

A parasite is a species that lives on ▶ another species, causing it harm. The cuckoo is a bird with a parasitic lifestyle. Rather than building her own nest, the female cuckoo lays eggs in nests built by smaller species, such as hedge sparrows or reed warblers. When the young cuckoo hatches, the first thing it does is push any other eggs or nestlings over the side. The poor unsuspecting foster parents are left with just one large mouth to feed.

Parasites cause many unpleasant and often fatal ▶ diseases in humans. Colds, chicken pox, mumps, and AIDS are caused by different kinds of viruses reproducing in the human body. A virus is a tiny particle, even smaller than a bacterium, containing hereditary material. It cannot reproduce on its own, so it is not strictly alive, but it takes over living cells and makes them produce copies of itself.

GROWING OLD

All living things eventually grow old and die. The records for long life are without doubt held by members of the plant kingdom. Yew trees can easily live for more than 1,000 years. The oldest known living tree is a bristle cone pine like the one in the picture. It is in California, and is 4,700 years old. ▶

Animals cannot match trees for length of life. Giant tortoises may live for up to 120 years, elephants and parrots for 70 to 80 years. The life expectancy for a man born in a developed country is now about 72 years; for a woman, it is 76 years.

Some creatures have very short lives. An adult mayfly lives for only a few hours after emerging from the water, just long enough to mate and lay eggs. The adult mayfly has no mouth parts and does not feed during its short life.

WOW! The oldest human being on record was Shigechiyo Izumi of Japan, who died on February 21, 1986, aged 120 years and 237 days.

As an animal gets older, changes take place in its body. Muscles get smaller, joints become stiffer, and the animal moves more slowly. And it's not just humans whose hair turns gray – so does the hair on other mammals, such as dogs and horses.

Older animals may not run as fast or jump as high, but they still have much to contribute to a group. The experience and skills they have gained from many years of life are passed on to new generations by the learning process. When they eventually die, they are not always just forgotten. If elephants come across elephant bones, they circle and trumpet almost as if they are mourning their dead relatives.

Individual animals die, and so can an entire species. When the last member of a species dies, the species is extinct. The causes of extinction may include disease, climate change, predators, and natural disasters. But the greatest threat to many species today is the destruction of their habitats by human beings.

Dinosaurs were the most successful group of animals ever. They ruled the earth for 160 million years. Then, 65 million years ago, the dinosaurs became extinct. The cause of their extinction remains one of the great mysteries of life. ▼

GLOSSARY

Adaptation   Any feature of a living thing that helps it to survive. For example, a penguin's thick blubber helps it survive the cold Antarctic weather.

Amphibian   An animal such as a frog that can live on land but lays its eggs in water.

Anthers   The male parts of a flower. They produce pollen.

Asexual reproduction Reproduction that does not involve mating between a male and a female.

Carnivore   An animal that eats other animals – a meat eater.

Chrysalis   A stage in the life cycle of the butterfly or moth in which the body develops under a hard shell covering.

Clone   An exact copy of a living thing. A clone has the same genes as the original.

Dispersal   The process by which seeds are spread. Some seeds are dispersed by the wind, others by animals.

DNA   (deoxyribonucleic acid) Microscopic chemical substance that forms the "code" of all life and determines what an organism will be like.

Embryo   The earliest stage of development after fertilization. For mammals, the baby is inside the mother; with other animals, the baby is inside an egg. Plant embryos also form after fertilization.

Evolution   Changes to living things that take place from generation to generation, eventually producing new species.

Extinct   When the last member of a species dies, the species is extinct.

Gene   The part of the DNA code in living things that determines a particular feature such as eye color.

Gill   The breathing organ of fish and other aquatic animals.

Herbivore   An animal that eats plants only.

Hereditary   Passed on from one generation to another.

Immune   Not affected by a certain type of disease.

Imprinting   The process by which some newborn animals become attached to a "parent." Goslings become attached to the first creature they see.

Instinct   Behavior that animals are born with as opposed to behavior that is learned. Breathing is an instinctive behavior.

Mammal   Any warm-blooded animal that feeds its young on milk. Humans, whales, mice, and bats are all mammals.

Metamorphosis   A process that some animals go through as they mature, in which their bodies change form. For example, a tadpole metamorphoses into a frog.

Molting   The process of shedding the exterior of certain animals, usually to replace the old shell, fur, feathers, or other skin.

Parasite   A living thing that lives on another living thing, usually doing it harm.

Photosynthesis   The process by which plants capture the energy of sunlight in their leaves.

Predator   An animal that hunts other animals for food.

Prey   Animals that are hunted and eaten by predators.

Protists   One of the five kingdoms of living things, protists are chiefly microscopic and one-celled; they consist of protozoa and some algae.

Reproduce   To produce offspring or young.

Reptile   Any cold-blooded animal with a scaly or plate-covered outer body, the young of which are produced in eggs. Snakes, lizards, crocodiles, turtles, and tortoises are all reptiles.

Respiration The process by which living things combine oxygen and food to produce energy.

Sexual reproduction Reproduction in which the male and female of a species mate. The offspring have a mixture of their parents' genes.

Symbiosis Two species living together in a way that benefits them both.

BOOKS TO READ

Baker, Wendy and Haslam, Andrew. *Insects*. Make it Work! New York: Thomson Learning, 1994.

Burnie, David. *How Nature Works: One Hundred Ways Parents and Kids Can Share the Secrets of Nature*. New York: Reader's Digest Association, 1991.

Haslam, Andrew. *Body*. Make it Work! New York: Thomson Learning, 1994.

Hemsley, William. *Feeding to Digestion: Projects with Biology*. Hands On Science. New York: Gloucester Press, 1992.

Margulis, Lynn. *Diversity of Life: The Five Kingdoms*. Hillside, NJ: Enslow Publishers, 1992.

Parker, Steve. *Nerves to Senses: Projects with Biology*. Hands On Science. New York: Gloucester Press, 1991.

Peacock, Graham and Hudson, Terry. *The Super Science Book of Our Bodies*. Super Science. Thomson Learning, 1993.

Twist, Clint. *Reproduction to Birth: Projects with Biology*. Hands On Science. New York: Gloucester Press, 1991.

INDEX